In Between The Lines

- Black Edition -

James McInerney

DEDICATION

Terri, Ethan and Erin – May you forever remain by my side.

CONTENTS

CONTENTS

CONTENTS

CONTENTS

CONTENTS

ACKNOWLEDGMENTS

First and foremost I would like to thank the two most important people in the whole wide world "Mum and Dad I love you". Thank you for being the best parents a boy could ever want, you taught me all the right things and I owe you the greatest debt of all.

Secondly I would like to thank my wife Terri who has constantly supported me and my works from the beginning and someone who has been a major part in the construction of this book. You are my world, forever and always.

Huge hugs and loads of love to my two children Ethan and Erin, who occasionally read my works and often show me poems they have written themselves. Future poets in the making I reckon.

A huge thank you to the amazingly awesome Helen Knott who was the first person to ever say 'Yes' and someone who continues to give me great advice when asked. I owe you so much.

To all the amazing staff at BBC Radio Northampton, who on numerous occasions have invited me into the studio to speak about my works. Thank you for making me feel at ease and allowing me to be myself so that I could say what I needed to say.

A massive thank you to all the magazines and their editors who over the years took a risk and featured me and my works, your support has made a huge difference. Emails have been sent to each and every one of you to say thank you.

Thank you to all the amazingly talented YouTube Artists who have turned my words into beautiful songs over the years. I have enjoyed the creative process with each and every one of you and made some amazing new friends along the way. May you find the success you so rightly deserve.

To all the members and the amazing admin team of 'Freedom Writers Ink' who over the years have opened my eyes to a world filled with poetry and showed me a love that will last forever. Thank you so much.

Thank you to all the Actors, Actresses and Radio DJ's who have lent their amazing voices to my words, you gave them a new lease of life that I never thought possible.

And of course thank you to all my friends and followers on Facebook and Twitter. Thank you for sharing, tweeting, liking and commenting on all my writes, you are the reason why I put pen to paper and do what I do.

"…..Love is everything, and yet it is nothing at all….."

TODAY NOT TOMORROW

Tomorrow's sky will never show,
Such Beauty as it did today,
The way the sun sets and rises,
Will happen in a different way,
The rain may fall again upon me,
Though it won't taste or feel the same,
The wind may be calm and gentle,
Yet it still won't recite your name,
The world will keep on turning,
As though it knew no other way,
It won't have realised how beautiful,
It was just yesterday.

RUST

My world is nothing but a lifetime of rust,
Every memory devoured as it's turned into dust,
My spirit once strong,
Now grows tired and weak,
As I dwell amongst the shadows,
Where the sun cannot reach.

And the people whom I pass as I walk through the streets,
Still wear hope upon their smiles,
With every breath that they breathe,
Unaware of the rust and how it grows deep within,
Slowly infecting their hearts,
Before it seeps through the skin.

And the stain that it leaves is but a reminder of life,
Every scar slowly carved by a sharp painful knife,
For this eternal tattoo comprised of torment and grief,
Never falters in its path,
Until you're brought to your knees.

But what I've learned through the years as time passes me by,
Is although it owns me now,
It can't when I die.
So on the fateful day when there's no strength left to lend,
I'll quietly lure it in,
Knowing the end,
Is…
The…
End…

ESPIRITO

From across the divide,
We shall finally meet,
Through the tunnel of light,
Where the angels sleep,
All the tears in your eyes,
May I kiss them away?
Because the smile you now hide,
Breaks my heart every day.

WALKING AMONGST ANGELS

My arm outstretched,
And with a guiding hand,
To touch the air,
To breathe the land,
The warmth of the sun,
Bright coloured raybeams bouncing off my face,
Solitude in my mind has always been a place.
Reality the experience of existence,
Feelings displayed to look but not to touch,
Emotions so clear you can read them like a book,
Do you see my inner lining?
It is woven with a twist,
And like all of those before you,
I now no longer exist.
Like a lone heart in an open minefield,
Quickly washing the tears away,
The truth becomes a vision,
So bright and full of promise in a way.
With feathered wings made of silk and of gold,
I am floating high above you,
Do you try and grab hold?
My breathing so shallow,
One heartbeat at a time,
My body so loose,
My pulse barely in line,
Is this heaven?
Or the end of mankind?
A family to leave,
But always in mind.
And if anyone should ask,
Or enquire of me,
Just tell them the story,
Of how it all went,
That I'm walking amongst angels,
And that I was heaven sent.

DEARLY DEPARTED

Your love will save me in the end,
Three simple words will on my life depend,
I'll tell you when with a final kiss,
The taste of your tears will never leave my lips.
And when the sky is no more,
And my breath doesn't hold,
Don't cry for me,
Don't bury your soul,
For in your arms my love for you hasn't died,
It has just begun,
Through you I will have survived.

MY BEAUTIFUL PALOMA

Paloma!
Paloma!
There's a fire inside you,
I'll forgive you your sins,
Because I know you were frightened.
You sacrificed your heart,
For the demons who required it,
In a moment of weakness,
It was your spirit that was blinded.

Do you hide amongst the shadows?
Another victim of violence,
Tell me where do you dwell?
Beneath the whispers and silence?
Or are you somewhere safe?
Where only lovers can find you.

I promise you this,
My beautiful Paloma,
I'll never let go,
Holding hands in the twilight,
For you live in us all,
By your courage,
We are guided.

KEEPER

I carry your love in my pocket,
I've done it all my life,
So scared that I could lose it,
I've always held it tight,
Sometimes I often wonder,
Although it would hurt to even know,
Would it find another pocket if I ever let it go?

THE LAST TIME I CRIED

I still remember the day like no time has passed,
And yet the wounds that cut me deep,
Are now a mass of hidden scars,
For the girl I used to be,
The one you brought down to her knees,
Exists where no one ever looks,
As her body slowly bleeds.

And the smile I always wore,
That used to fill my life with hope,
Is but a noose around my neck,
Whilst I dangle from the rope,
And though I tried to Carry on and accept the life I found,
The rope grows shorter every day,
Gaining distance from the ground.

And with every painful breath,
Oh how I kick and grab the air,
Having to fight life on my own,
When there's no one else who cares.
Forced to give into my fate with a motionless retreat,
The taste of poison on my lips,
The darkness clawing at my feet.
And all the angels up above,
In their glorious domain,
May they close their eyes in sorrow,
As they hang their heads in shame.

Why didn't you listen to the words I screamed?
As they poured out of my mouth,
Or see the tears stream down my face,
In a silent plea for help,
All of the times I begged and begged,
And yet you didn't even hear,
Pinning my arms down by my sides,
Whilst you punished me with fear.
Why couldn't you stop for just a second?
And see the mess you made,
I never believed in faith or religion,
But every night I prayed and prayed.

"Oh God please make it stop!...."

And I'm reminded of the pain even to this very day,
For the girl I used to be,
Got left behind and lost her way,
And though I often call her name,
Just to check if she's ok,
She only responds to me with silence,
Like there's nothing left to say.

And the tears you made her cry,
The day her whole world slowly died,
I still wear them to remind me,
Of the last time that I cried.

AUTUMN LEAVES

I'm but an autumn leaf upon the ground,
A remnant of all summers past,
The ember sun above me shines,
To warm me on my bed of grass.
My golden skin,
Now Paper thin,
Moves in rhythm with the wind,
And though I have no place to call my home,
I still belong to where the seasons roam.
Be it summer,
Winter,
Spring,
Or fall,
Regardless of the time of day,
Oh how I dance amongst a sea of souls,
Unafraid of change that comes my way,
And though the years may differ each time around,
I'll forever be an autumn leaf upon the ground.

DO I LOVE THEE TOO MUCH?

If your love shall be an anchor,
To sit upon my heart,
Then every look upon your face,
I am punished from the start.

TOO MANY WHAT IFS

What if you loved, or if you cared, or even dared?
What if your heart didn't start when you stared?
What if your mind couldn't stop thinking of me?
What if you knew it but you just couldn't see?
What if it happened then how would you feel?
What if the thoughts in your head became real?
What if you loved me if only the once?
And pictured the future being us?
What if I wrote this to remind you of me?
What if it worked?
Then where would we be?

OH THUNDEROUS SKY

Oh thunderous sky,
I'm dancing beneath you,
The wind in my hair,
As I hide in the shadows.
Although you are dark,
I don't want to leave you,
You make me feel safe,
As you look down upon me.
Your soft talking sounds,
How they echo inside me,
It's like when you speak,
I'm consumed in a heartbeat.
In its jealous rage,
I know the light would defy you,
I'd curse it in spite,
Screaming "I don't even like you!"
In your presence I'm lost,
I hope that nobody finds me,
Amongst the darkness we'll dwell,
Eternally silent.

ASPIRE

Go find your soul wherever it may be,
Let the words upon your tongue,
Be the ones that set you free,
Let the hope inside your heart,
Prolong the thoughts that you may have,
And the courage that you will find,
Will be something full of love.

DO YOU STILL LOVE ME?

Is your heart for sale?
Or is it already sold?
Did they pay you in love?
Or pay you in gold?
Are the words so sacred?
That they've never been yours?
Was I your reprieve last night?
Or was I something more?

RAPTURE

Oh Rapturous spirit how I watch you dance,
Through the sky you glide with elegance,
Untouched by pain,
Overwhelmed by love,
Your chains of hate,
Have come undone.

Oh Rapturous spirit so divine and free,
Come dance this way,
Come dance with me.

SURVIVE

Are you my sanctuary here?
All my hopes,
My desires,
So scared that I could surrender myself,
If I thought you'd reply.
The whole of my heart,
For one piece of your sky,
In this place that I dwell,
Amongst the tears that I've cried.
Please don't tell me you love me,
As you whisper goodbye,
For tonight I'm in heaven,
Beneath the stars,
I reside.

PRETTY VACANT

Just down the hall,
Towards the door on the left,
At the bottom of the stairs,
Amongst all the books on the shelves.
In the cold empty kitchen,
Where the light dare not dwell,
In the heart of our home,
That still carries your scent.
The unfinished meal,
Sits patiently still,
So innocent,
So loving,
It longs to exist.
The warmth of the sunrise,
By the house on the lake,
The words that were left unspoken,
The ones we meant to say.
The place where the rain fell,
Washing all the tears from your eyes,
The night the world stood still,
As one of its angels died.
These are the places,
Our love now remains,
I visit them always,
In case the memories fade.
I'm haunted by silence,
And all the pain that it brings,
Consumed by its darkness,
Denied of my dreams.

SOUL MATE
~ For Terri ~

Your name recited upon my heart,
Whispered softly by our unborn child,
The gods of love have set out your fate,
And shared it with my mind.

Our destiny on parallel paths,
Memories treasured new and old,
United at one final point,
Linked eternal,
Soul to soul.

WINGS OF LOVE

Love is like a fairytale,
You gave it wings,
The day you smiled,
My eyes were closed,
I could not see,
An angel standing next to me.

Upon silent breath and mortal tongue,
It took the pain that made me numb,
With a broken heart I dare not break,
I still dream of you,
Afraid I'll wake.

EVERYTHING

I am everything,
And yet I'm nothing at all,
I am tomorrow's dawn,
Before the mornings call.
I am here with you,
Even when you're alone,
I am love,
I am hope,
I am skin and bone.
I am all the things,
That pass you by,
So stop,
And breathe,
And take the time … to know me.

ACCEPTANCE

These scars of woven ink I wear,
Leave their marks upon my skin,
For every cut I've had to bear,
Reminds me of the pain love brings,
And though I've tried with all my heart,
To erase the sorrow from my past,
In time I know there will come a day,
I'll regain the strength life took away.

WHILE I SLEEP

Take me in your arms and hold me while I sleep,
Your fingers interlocked in mine,
Like the perfect dream,
The softness of your skin up close,
The words you speak so sweet,
You probably didn't realise this,
You made me feel complete.

PASSING

~ Dedicated to Mary Teresa McInerney ~

The news comes so sudden,
There's no time to reflect,
Or think,
Or speak,
Only time to regret.
Your name I always knew,
But your face I forget,
I'm sorry,
Forgive me,
I'm trying my best.

I shall arrive in my colours,
And bid you farewell,
I shall smile at all the people,
And listen to the stories they tell,
I shall shake all their hands,
And feel out of place,
I shall do the right thing and remember your face.

May your journey ahead be loving and safe,
Your home is your heart,
In your resting place.

"Sleep tight…"

SHADOW

My spirit is but a shadow,
My soul a ray of light,
My mind a perfect day,
My body a perfect night.

ANGEL IN MY ROOM

There's an angel in my room,
Stood where no one else can see,
Existing just beyond the silence,
Of an early morning breeze.
It often talks to me in whispers,
And places thoughts inside my head,
So that every time I close my eyes,
I'm somewhere else instead.
And I never feel alone,
When I know it's close nearby,
For every tear I used to own,
Is placed on clouds up in the sky,
So that every time it rains,
All my pain is washed away,
And I smile because I know,
That regardless of the day,
There's an angel in my room,
And in my room,
Is where it'll stay.

DARK CLOUDED VEIL

I wear a dark clouded veil,
That consumes the air I breathe,
Making every breath I used to take,
So much harder to achieve.
And beneath this veil so dark,
All my thoughts are not my own,
For I am forced to grieve in silence,
Whilst I walk this path alone.
And the sun that used to shine,
Through the clouds up in the sky,
Is now a mist of discontent,
Like a fog before my eyes,
Until I am blinded by the memories,
The ones I used to own of you,
Beneath my dark clouded veil,
Trapped within a world bereft of view.

BORN BROKEN

I wish you were older,
So you could understand,
Why it's easier to give in,
Then to reach for your hand.
You know nothing of feelings and emotional scars,
Or how love can destroy,
As it rips you apart.
It's like a disease,
Slowly infecting the heart,
As it moves to your head,
Where it finishes you off.

I'm so glad you can't hear me,
When I cry in the bath,
Reaching out in the water,
Eyes closed to the dark,
Or how quick I shut down,
When people get real close,
Too scared they would see,
That my smiles just for show,
And that inside I'm slowly dying,
Just another victim of this world,
For it's not always by fire,
That we end up getting burnt.

HOME

~ Written for and Inspired by Terri ~

"You are with me always…I can feel it…I can feel you…."

If I cannot find you in this life,
Bound eternal by a love so strong,
That even angels couldn't comprehend its beauty,
Then I shall look to my heart to show me the way.

If 'Love' shall be my compass,
Then you will be my guide,
My one true north,
The place where I feel safe.

And if I get lost along the way,
May my faith in hope point me towards you,
For you are my final destination,
You are my way home.

LADY BY THE LAKE

My lady by the lake,
Still searches for her sea,
And dreams of summers past,
Amongst the innocence of trees.
Their leaves have now all fallen,
Quietly stolen by the breeze,
Yet there lives in her a sadness,
As all the colours start to bleed.
Held hostage by the shadows,
I watch her slowly grieve,
Helplessly I wait,
Learning how to breathe,
For I know she'll find the courage,
When it comes the time to leave,
And I'll be waiting just beyond the sunrise,
With all the love she'll ever need.

FOREVER

I fear the darkness,
The way that it fills me with dread,
And as much as I hide,
It still feeds on my scent.
I bleed every day,
Like a victim of desire,
I'm a casualty of passion,
My freedom denied.
And as it holds me captive,
Cruelly delaying the end,
As much as I hate it,
It's my only friend.

1977

Pariah! Pariah!
I'd sell my soul for your fire,
You open my eyes,
And make me dream of desire.
Tempted by lust,
I surrender complete,
One taste of your lips,
And I'm brought to my knees.

Pariah! Pariah!
I crave what you offer,
With my mortal remains,
I'll be a sinner amongst lovers,
Devouring the weak,
And watching them suffer,
Eyes closed to the world,
I'm consumed by your Hunger.

TRYING TO REMEMBER

I still close my eyes,
To remember your face,
And write your name next to mine,
In every empty space,
Too scared that if I stop,
You'll slowly fade away,
In my lonely little room,
That consumes me every day.

OH TO BE A BIRD

Oh to be a bird,
And dwell in the sky,
With the wind beneath my wings,
I'd watch the world from up on high,
Then I wouldn't feel so lonely,
And I'd never have to cry,
Because there'd be no one to disown me,
And forget that I'm alive.

Oh to be a bird,
With the freedom of flight,
Knowing I could soar up towards heaven,
Whenever I liked,
To a place filled with angels,
Who would lend me their light,
So I could pretend that I was special,
Instead of always feeling despised.

Oh to be a bird,
How I wish I could fly,
Never having to look through the window,
With all these tears in my eyes,
Hoping one day they will listen,
And not shout all the time,
Then this pain wouldn't want me,
And I could learn how to smile.

Oh to be a bird,
And live in the clouds,
Knowing I would stay there forever,
Too afraid to come down!

THE BEAUTY OF TREES

If I should fall by the wayside,
Beyond the length of your reach,
Do not think of me in sorrow,
With every tear you gently weep,
Because you'll never walk alone,
On the road that lays ahead,
For I am the breeze amongst the trees,
That overlook the path you tread.

ALIVE

You give me hope,
When I own nothing but grief,
On a cold winters day,
You're the warmth that I seek,
Consumed by sorrow,
You allow me to speak,
And though I hate that I hide it,
It's all I can do just to breathe.

I still cry every time that you leave,
Wanting more from each moment,
Instead of a life fuelled by tears,
Never knowing if it's all but a dream,
Holding onto the memories,
Till the next time we meet.

Can't you tell that these feelings run deep?
Why won't you look into my eyes and see how I see?
Am I so obvious to the point of retreat?
Still afraid of the silence,
And these wounds that won't bleed.

May the darkness devour me complete,
Slowly infecting my heart,
Till I learn of defeat,
Like a hostage,
I await my release,
Because if you can't tell me you love me,
I can never be free.

COMFY PLACE

All wrapped up and warm,
Protected from hate,
The big bad world,
Won't see me today,
These dangerous people,
Again I'll escape,
Another day,
In my comfy place.

I'M ALONE INSIDE
IN EVERY SINGLE WAY

I'm alone inside in every single way,
Caught between the darkness of the night,
And the emptiness of day.
And though I always scream so loud,
You never seem to hear a word I say,
Trapped behind this invisible wall of glass,
My sorrow like a hostage on display.
And every tear upon my face,
Is how I'm reminded of you,
Wearing these scars upon my skin,
Forced to cover every painful bruise,
But what you probably didn't know,
Every time you knocked me down,
Is how much it hurt that I couldn't un-love you,
Even whilst you were pinning me to the ground.

And I prayed with all my heart,
That god could make you want to change,
Hanging onto all the times you made me smile,
To try and block out all the pain,
For even as the taste of my own blood,
Slowly gathered in my mouth,
I never faltered in my devotion,
Or lent my mind to doubt,
Because I knew deep down inside,
Underneath your burning rage,
That you were just as scared as I was,
But you chose to hide it all away.

You punished every part of me,
For all the words you couldn't say,
Until the silence turned to violence,
And you forced our love away.
And although I've said goodbye,
If only for a while,
I still fear every empty moment,
When I can't feel you by my side.
And the world will never know,
Regardless of the day,
How much I'm alone inside in every single way.

ESPERANZA (HOPE)

Whilst in your arms I could just die,
Never knowing where or how or why,
In your thoughts may I always be,
Every smile your reflection of me.

NUMB

Hope in a world without meaning,
Is how my heart feels every time that you leave me,
The tears in your eyes they stain me so,
Like a cross everlasting,
You mark my soul,
And to no one else no matter how hard I try,
I can never ever fully explain why.

I DARE YOU

I dare you to love me with what's in your heart,
To open your eyes and come out of the dark.
I dare you to want me when were up real close,
And not pull away like your scared it will show.
I dare you to feel it when I kiss you goodbye,
When the tears in your eyes show your hurting inside.
I dare you to tell me that your feelings are real,
Like when I look at you there's always one thing I fear,
That I'll let you go and you'll disappear.

"I dare you"

I beg you to dare me back!

ASSASSIN OF LOVE

I'm an army of lovers,
In a sea full of souls,
I am loves true assassin,
Amongst the shadows I roam,
With hope in my heart,
And hate upon my breath,
I dine with the devil,
And all of its friends!

SENSORY

I love the way your hand,
Fits to the shape of mine,
Our fingers interlocked,
It's like we become lost for a while.
No more interruptions,
Just the warmth of your smile,
And whenever I'm with you,
You make me realise who I really am inside.
For In your arms I am home,
Like a stolen lovers kiss,
You consume my every heartbeat,
And fill my soul with bliss.

EROS

For my wings I have no use,
To reach heaven I need neither fly nor soar,
But instead fall,
Fall in love.

SPIRAL

Oh what a vicious web we weave,
On devils breath and tongue we bleed,
As our world begins its slow demise,
On muted lips may only our souls survive.

Oh wicked heart how you taint me still,
Although the silence is always worse I fear,
Just before the kill.

MONO-TYPE

Oh lonely little girl,
Slowly dying in the snow,
Your skin all black and blue,
Paints a picture of this world.
Your raven red hair stained,
Hides the face that no one knew,
All curled up in a ball,
I bet that no one's missing you.

Are you black?
Or are you white?
Does it really matter now?
For as you lay all on your own,
It shouldn't be the colour of your skin,
That lets you down.

Oh tiny little child,
Your eyes as dark as death,
You've held the hands of strangers,
Hoping love would be your friend.
I'll take you from this place,
But be careful where you tread,
Because something needs to change,
When we can be better off dead!

EMILY

My love for you is lost,
As the sea departs the shore,
Frozen by the tide,
Upon the sand that we once walked.
The stars up in the sky,
Have lost the grace they held before,
I still search for you each night,
Bound forever,
Wanting more.

BEAUTY

I dare not define beauty so,
For the definition of beauty be that not of the sky above,
But that of a feeling,
A feeling of emotions that are worth more than the stars and the moon,
They are priceless,
Not available to barter with or sell,
They are a poor man's dream,
I am poor,
Therefore I dream.

THE CORNFIELD

As I stand here alone in this cornfield,
The almost silent humming sound of the wind,
Blows through my hair and all around me,
The golden corn gently lashing from side to side,
Keeps in rhythm with the wind,
And the glowing sun warms alongside my face.
I have never seen anything so beautiful before in my life,
And yet I close my eyes,
The wind around me I sway gently back and forth,
Each time breathing out as though it were my last,
Every breath a part of me.

I can feel my heartbeat slowing down now,
Matching alongside the pace of the wind,
Gentle and calm,
And with my eyes closed I extend out both of my arms,
Gently tilting back my head.
The slow gusts of wind wash over the palms of my hands,
And the curves of my face,
Coexisting in perfect harmony,
Slowly but carefully warming my heart,
Touching every single emotion inside of me.
And with my body rendered powerless I fall down to my knees,
The corn cradling me as I fall,
Holding me tight to protect me,
Shielding me from danger.

Suddenly the wind stops,
Everything is quiet and so peaceful now,
No more sounds just silence.
I open my eyes and look up into the clear blue sky above me,
And with an open mind,
Free from confusion or doubt,
I realise this is where I belong now,
I am at home here in this cornfield,
And although I am all alone,
I have never felt so complete.

SOMEWHERE BETWEEN
LOVE AND HATE

I think I died,
I think I'm dead,
The darkness came,
And took my breath.
In whispers now I only speak,
Denied of love,
Required to bleed.

Oh heaven,
How you hold me still,
As I hide amongst your paper hearts,
This morbid curse of tongue and breath,
Devours all angels in its path.

My hand outstretched,
Consumed by death,
Please let me go,
It's for the best!

CARRY YOU HOME

I will carry you home,
Even though you have gone,
And honour your life,
With a beautiful song.
I'd sing it so loud,
Like I was speaking to god,
Returning one of his angels,
For the promise of love.
And until heaven finds me,
I shall never let go,
Holding hope in my arms,
So the whole world can know,
How much I love you.

ZEA

My beautiful Zea,
Since the day you were born,
I gave you something special,
That will forever be yours.

It has lived inside of me,
All of this time,
And I'm reminded of its presence,
When I look in your eyes.

I have given you a gift,
Even money can't buy,
That sits upon your heart,
And in the warmth of your smile.

I will pray every day,
'Zea' my child,
The love you now have,
May it keep you alive.

PERFECT

If your heart can be portrayed,
Through a look or a stare,
Then gaze into my eyes,
Whilst I kiss you there.

BEAUTIFUL DAY

You died on a beautiful day,
All the angels appeared,
And they took you away.
The sun was out shining,
Not a cloud in the sky,
The children were playing,
Their hearts full of life.
The world showed more colour,
As you said your goodbyes,
And although you are gone,
I know you're not far away,
For I shall see you again,
On a beautiful day.

FALLEN

My tiny little flower,
We have so much in common,
You're alone in this world,
Because nobody listens.

You look to the sky,
And ask it for answers,
But it never replies,
So you sit in the darkness.

Your leaves become weak,
Demanding attention,
I wish I could help,
But I've no strength left to mention.

Consumed by the silence,
Were on similar paths,
Another victim of violence,
Protecting its heart.

IF I COULD......I WOULD

If I could paint you a picture,
I would create it from your smile,
Your beauty would become my colours,
The passion reflected in your eyes.

If I could compose you a sonnet,
It would only sing out your name,
And when the lonely hearts listened,
I would share with them my pain.

FUERZA

Pull me under and never let go,
For I would swim in all your rivers,
If I thought they'd take me home.
My heart has lost its keeper,
And the memories it used to own,
The feelings you have left me,
I now share them without knowing.
You've denied me of my pleasures,
With all the promises you break,
You keep on burning all my butterflies,
Upon every breath you dare to take.
I refuse to go to sleep,
To pay for your mistakes,
If I am going to die alone,
I shall do it whilst I wake!

TOUCH THE SKY

Touch the sky,
Let it know what you have to bring,
Make your mark,
Force the world to its feet!

LOVE IS BLIND

Love is but an illusion,
That exists within the mind,
For as it opens up your eyes,
Oh how it's visions leave you blind,
And I have looked upon its face,
Way too many times,
But I can't escape the pain,
Of how it hurts that it's not mine.

THE PRICE OF LOVE

Oh forgive me lord,
For I have sinned,
Recklessly pursuing the heart of another,
Whilst harbouring the hope of a dream,
Knowing that the promise of love,
The one thing I can never ignore,
Will always repay me in sorrow,
Destroying all the things I hold dear.
And every memory I treasured,
That time slowly steals,
Leaves marks upon my skin,
That take an eternity to heal,
Like a constant reminder,
So that I can never be free,
For come tomorrow when the sun shines,
And there sits a smile upon my face,
The world will never know that on the inside,
How I'm bereft of loves embrace.

BEFORE THE STORM

When the lights go down,
And I'm standing all alone,
The whole world solemn at my feet,
To gently remind me that you're gone,
I'll ignore the sounds of silence,
Whilst they echo through my ears,
And pray to god and the heavens above,
To save me from these tears.

AT THE WATER'S EDGE

At the water's edge,
Is where I now stand,
Its jagged rocks,
My innocence,
For the love I used to own before,
Is but a poison within my veins,
Awaiting the cure.
And the tides of time that leave their mark,
Consume my soul within an instant,
Turning everything dark,
Until I'm nothing but a memory,
That slowly fades without thought,
Washed away by the waves,
Denied my 'Hand of support'.
And the tears that I've cried,
The ones that nobody saw,
Shall become my constant companion,
Whilst I stand at the shore,
For at the water's edge,
I shall always be,
Unnoticed,
Unwanted,
Slowly devoured by the sea.

FAITHFULLY DEVOTED

Oh dearest forever after,
Whoever you may be,
I shall walk this world a stranger,
Until you finally notice me,
And though I've never kissed your lips,
Or held you in my arms,
Or explained to you the way I feel,
In the hope you'd understand,
I will never lose my faith,
As I live and breathe each day,
For I won't find another 'You',
And that's the way it'll always stay.

DIRTY PRETTY THING

Oh painted heart,
You are blind to the dangers,
Indulging in deeds,
As you associate with strangers.
Your foreign tongue,
Now leaves you all tainted,
Accepting desire as your sin,
Yet in its presence you are jaded.
I'll liberate your soul,
If that's what you need,
Just one taste from my lips,
And you'll wake from this dream.

THRIVE

I was born amongst strangers,
But died amongst friends,
It's the feeling of belonging,
That saves you in the end.

BABEL

I have to force myself,
To forget your face,
Because with every waking breath,
Begins another empty day.
As I surrender the memories,
I've collected for years,
Somehow the feelings still linger,
Amongst the taste of your tears.
Consumed by denial,
Betrayed by regret,
A handful of dreams,
Are all I have left.
I'm broken inside,
With no more words left to say,
I shared them with love once,
But when it came,
It took them all away!

LONG WALK HOME

We all move forward,
In the same direction,
Our whole lives spent searching,
For one glimpse of affection.

Paths will be crossed,
All the memories forgotten,
Yet the further we walk,
Still the pain doesn't lessen.

The journey may be long,
But we are never alone,
And deny as we might,
We all have our long walk home.

And though I can feel you beside me,
With every step that I take,
Regardless of the distance,
I shall find you someday.

FOREVER IN LOVE

I'm always reminded how you smiled when I held you,
And closed your eyes because I made you feel safe,
I'd rather be loved by you whilst I'm still dreaming,
Then be denied when my bodies awake.
I still remember your taste as you kissed me,
And the pain in your tears that pushed you away,
I promise to love you forever my angel,
Please tell me that it's not too late!

JEREMIAH DELANEY

Once upon a silent grave,
I met a man who knew my name,
He told a tale as old as time,
Made up with memories from my mind.
He played a tune that matched his words,
And with every note,
The pain got worse,
I couldn't speak,
My voice was gone,
My words were stolen by his song.
He danced beneath the midnight dusk,
With eyes of black,
And teeth of rust,
My final breath he took from me,
I saw him smile,
I watched his glee.
I should have known,
Right from the start,
When you meet 'Jeremiah Delaney',
Always be careful of your heart.

TAKEN

With arms out wide,
And eyes that sleep,
The darkness came,
And stole from me.

I wake each night,
But you're not here,
I cannot cry another tear.

Tell me where was my god?
When I begged for his help,
That he could take you from me,
Instead of somebody else.

I'll never forgive him,
Or speak of his name,
My faith is forgotten,
And I've replaced it with pain.

What I kept in my heart,
Has been taken away,
For a life without love,
Is like night without day,
And if we sacrifice too much,
There'll be nothing left in us to save.

A PROMISE

~ Written for Terri ~

I pledge to you a promise,
Of my heart and of my soul,
The warmth you've put inside of me,
That makes me feel whole.

I promise to be true to you,
To make you smile when you are sad,
To give to you everything,
That you thought you'd never have.

I promise to protect you,
To never let you go,
To hold you close in my arms,
So you'll always know.

I promise to share with you,
All these feelings that I have,
My love for you will never change,
Promise me,
You'll love me back!

HOLDING ON

Oh Lonely heart,
You're all I have,
A memory of a life I've lived,
Now silence is my only friend,
It numbs the pain,
I cannot mend.

I think of you like you're still here,
A dream from which I'll never wake,
These people who we called our friends,
They don't believe a word I say.

I tell them that you talk to me,
And all the stories that we share,
They look at me with sullen smiles,
I watch them leave,
"Does no one care?"

I think they're growing tired of me,
A feeling that I've felt for years,
I often sense their disbelief,
As to why I've always spared my tears.

I dare not tell them that I've lied,
About all the things I've said,
To admit that you've already died,
Would mean that you are dead,
And then I would have nothing left,
So I shall live a lie instead.

SOMEONE ELSE'S ADDICTION

Am I the latest addiction that you crave with your heart?
Because I can feel your warmth inside me,
Even when we are apart!

Desire is the poison,
That you use like a drug,
Infecting your victims,
Tainting their blood.

I won't let you destroy me,
I will fight until the end,
I'm nobody's 'something',
Don't you understand?

I'll deny you your pleasures,
Just to settle the score,
You'll have to beg me for forgiveness,
So I can want you even more!

GROUND RULES (GIRL POWER)

Let's make things clear,
Before we start,
I do have a brain,
And it talks to my heart.

My bodies my own,
Its mine to keep,
I'm with you right now,
But I can easily leave.

Do I look like a trophy?
You can share with your friends,
Please don't make that mistake,
Because that's when the relationship ends.

You could never know how I'm feeling,
Not all of the time,
I'm a complicated person,
So there's no point in trying.

If I tell you "No",
I still might mean "Yes"
Don't assume you know the answer,
Just by having a guess.

And when we make love,
Don't forget where you sleep,
When you look into my eyes,
You'd better be thinking of me.

I don't ask for much,
Just the occasional treat,
But if you buy me a gift,
Always keep the receipt.

If you stick by these rules,
Whenever you're with me,
I will love you forever,
That's a guarantee!

UNINVITED

I want this to be over,
Even before it's begun,
You can't hurt me anymore,
Because I'm already numb!

I will close my eyes,
And take all your pain,
Knowing the love in my heart,
Has been hidden away.

Though my body may be here,
I'm somewhere else in my head,
You can't destroy someone's Angel,
When it's already dead.

I hope that one day,
You will take it too far,
And finish me off properly,
So I don't have to hide another scar.

You're no longer a man,
Of that I'm sure,
Because If I had any strength left,
I wouldn't take this anymore.

LOST

I'm so close to the edge,
That I don't care if I fall,
Because if there's no one around,
Does it really matter at all?

They don't hear me when I'm crying,
Or feel the pain in my heart,
And there's no point in even trying,
When I don't know where to start.

I keep praying that an angel,
Will save me from my fate,
All I ever asked for was your loving,
But all you've given me is hate!

CRYING IN THE RAIN

I only cry when it rains,
To hide my tears whilst I weep,
Wearing this false smile upon my face,
Distracts from the scars deep beneath,
Like when you declared your true love,
But forgot to mention my name,
I remember not being able to breathe for a second,
Unable to deal with the pain,
Knowing I'd gave you all that I had,
With every inch of my soul,
You may have made me a woman,
But nothing can replace what you stole.
And this young girl inside of me,
Whoever she became,
Is all I hold onto for comfort,
Whilst I cry in the rain,
Another victim,
Amongst the nameless,
Is now where I remain.

TEMPTATION

I don't sleep well at night,
Unless I'm held in your arms,
When our bodies are up close,
In an instant I'm calm.

One taste of your skin,
And all the pleasures combine,
I need you inside me,
Because it feels so divine.

And when it's all over,
I shall dream with a smile,
Knowing the next time I wake,
You'll be right by my side,
And then I'll want you again,
Even though you're not mine!

BOUND

In a room full of faces,
In a sea full of souls,
May your eyes look upon me,
Even though they are closed.

IN DREAMS

I'd Search for you forever,
If it meant that you would stay,
I'm consumed by all these feelings,
That taunt me every day.

I'm devoured in every effort,
Denied of your embrace,
As I try to remember all the words,
That I never dared to say.

You're in my thoughts,
Throughout the day,
And even whilst I sleep,
I can feel inside,
The pain love brings,
And how a heart can bleed.

Every person that I look upon,
Reminds me of your face,
It's like you're getting closer still,
With every breath I take.

I know you're out there somewhere,
And I pray to god you're safe,
If dreams are all I have of you,
Then I shall never dare to wake.

CRUSHED

Close your mind to possibility,
Fill your life with hate,
Manipulate my feelings,
Apparently they don't really count.
Push away everyone you ever cared about,
The bitterness from deep inside is clawing its way out.
Bully me and bruise me,
If that's all your about,
I'll try and find it in my heart,
Not to scream and shout.
The truth is that I care too much,
Together we must fight,
This cancerous disease you have,
That's eating up your life!
Although you may not know this,
Through the trouble and the strife,
I need you here my one true love,
Don't quit,
Stand up and fight!

I MET AN ANGEL

I met an angel once,
And it shared with me the world,
I learned about forgiveness,
As it taught me how to love,
Its wings were not of feathers,
Nor covered all in gold,
But when it spoke,
I heard your voice,
And I knew that I was home.

I met an angel once,
And it whispered in my ear,
As it held me tight,
I closed my eyes,
And it wiped away my tears,
For I never knew what love was like,
Until an angel came to me.

ENDURING LOVE

Upon my last breath may I be punished no more!
If your love be that of a sword so strong and forgiving,
Then let it strike my heart with a mortal blow.
Alas worry not my dear,
For no marks or scars will appear across my skin,
Your beauty bestows no pain upon this body that lay before you,
And contempt dare not dwell here.
May your name be whispered upon my dying lips like that of dreams,
Where beauty resides knowing loves true form.

CRAVINGS

Give me an emotion,
I don't care which kind,
I need something I can cling to,
That occupies my mind.
Share with me your feelings,
Like you've known me all my life,
Inside my body taunts me,
As it craves you every night,
For bound to you I am empty,
Yet without you,
I'd surely die.

DREAMS

If dreams are made up of this,
The way our fingers interlock as we kiss,
Then I pray every night when I sleep,
All my dreams will come true,
And we will meet.

If memories are made up of love,
The way that you hold me so close when we hug,
Then all I can think of is you,
And the hope in my heart will stay true.

If heaven and angels exist,
You had better return,
As I know you'll be missed.

FORGOTTEN

The old man sits in silence,
Like he's waiting to die,
With his possessions already counted,
He watches the world pass him by.

Holding onto the memories,
Of when he was but a child,
With his wife long departed,
They're what keep him alive.

He feels no more sorrow,
For he's already said his goodbyes,
And doesn't dream of tomorrow,
Every time that he closes his eyes.

His now vacant expression,
Was once a beautiful smile,
With no more words left to mention,
It's just a matter of time.

APOCALYPSE

Oh Heavenly father,
Please forgive me my sins,
This poison inside me,
Is now all that remains.

I don't dream of your heaven,
Because it doesn't exist,
And I've destroyed too many angels,
To earn a place on your list.

When every teardrop can be stolen,
By the weight of the world,
Your compassion hides in silence,
So it can never be heard.

For every life that you take,
Another soldier is born,
There's an army inside us,
With its heart set on war.

I shall burn all your bibles,
So your words can't be read,
There will be a new religion,
Because the old one is dead!

WHITE PICKET FENCE

I've seen the world beyond the confines,
Of your White Picket Fence,
And tasted a freedom,
I could believe in,
Without the trappings of expense,
For life in all its glory,
Doesn't come at a price,
It's a present,
That you treasure,
That proves you're alive.

I DIED TODAY

"May our fondest memories become the ones that
save us in the end"

I died today,
And it's like you never even knew,
That as I breathed my last breath,
All I could think of was you.
Whispering final farewells,
Oh how I felt so alone,
Knowing there'd be no one to cling onto,
That would remind me of home.
And as I cried out in grief,
Hoping god would reply,
Sorrow streaming down my face,
Accepting the moment I'd die,
I saw you my darling,
And suddenly everything changed,
For all the pain that once owned me,
Gently faded away.
And the longing that lived in the depths of my soul,
The one that would always tear at my heart strings,
Reviving the memories of old,
It left me in an instant,
Whilst I gazed in your eyes,
Leaving such a warmth in my body that I couldn't deny.

Feeling hope in my veins,
For the very first time,
And the taste of your lips,
As they pressed against mine,
I reached out my hand,
Across the darkened divide,
Relying solely on faith,
And the will to survive,
Only to find you weren't where I thought you would be,
But in your place,
Stood a mirror,
Wearing a reflection of me.
And I knew in an instant,
Without the words being said,
That the illusion of promise,
Was born from the thoughts in my head,
Allowing me the strength that I needed,
To erase all these tears that I've wept,
Bereft of worry and fear,
And the courage to accept....
"I died today"

OH BETHLEHEM

Oh Bethlehem,
My sacred land,
I worship on your holy ground,
You speak to me,
In foreign tongue,
My mortal breath,
My rising sun.

I'm guided by your loving hand,
You give me strength,
When no one can,
My faith in you is absolute,
This path I walk,
Leads back to you.

INVISIBLE ME

I'm invisible,
The kind of invisible that no one ever sees,
It's like my words can't find their voice,
Every time I dare to speak.
And my friends who knew me well,
The ones who swore they'd never leave,
Are but a distant train of thought,
That's becoming harder to achieve,
Until I can barely breathe at all,
As people pass me on the street,
Their bodies blocking my every move,
Controlled by eyes that cannot see.
And I know they hear my voice,
As they step out of my way,
Pretending to look in a different direction,
Just to avoid the words they'll never say.

Oh heaven where are your angels now?
As I'm dragged down to the depths of my knees,
Do they not care enough to help?
Whilst they watch me quietly grieve,
Trapped in a world that prays for help,
And somehow still refuses to believe,
For invisible am I,
As I walk this path unknown,
One day I'll have to close my eyes forever,
But tell me who will notice that I have gone?

WANTED

There will never come a day,
When I do not dream of you,
Or watch the morning sunrise,
Amongst a perfect sky of blue.

My heart it may be broken,
Its hope devoured by every bruise,
But to deny the way I'm feeling,
Is like believing in the truth.

You gave me an emotion,
Knowing I'd embrace it with my love,
And treasure every moment,
From the second that we touched.

With a distance that divides us,
By all the words we've left unsaid,
I now find myself belonging,
To a place I can't forget.

Holding hands beneath the twilight,
Another victim of neglect,
I'm trapped by all the memories,
Of every tear I've ever wept.

GUARDIAN ANGEL

My beautiful child,
Your life needs to change,
Because I can't shield you from this world,
When you refuse to be saved.

To take the pain from your heart,
Knowing it's the one thing you crave,
Will drain every ounce of your courage,
So you'll have to be brave.

I know things may seem hopeless,
And that you're feeling afraid,
But I made a promise to protect you,
So I wouldn't have to cry at your grave.

Please don't become another victim,
As your soul slips away,
Take all the strength from my love,
And by your side I shall remain.

HEARTS HOME

Don't forget the stars for they carry you home,
And have lived in your heart since the day you were born,
We're strangers now,
But only for a while,
When the cycle restarts I'll be back by your side,
You'll love me then,
No more tears will I cry,
For we met in a place,
Only angels reside.

THE MOMENT HEAVEN STOLE MY TEARS AWAY

I awoke again today,
To an empty house,
Denied all the memories from my past,
Like they belonged to someone else.
And the pain that I felt,
Oh how it tore into my heart,
Reliving the moment I found forever,
Only to have heaven steal it from my arms.
And all the tears I couldn't cry,
The ones that never even came,
Still haunt me every single time,
I hear the mention of your name,
For when I close my eyes at night,
I still pretend that you're not gone,
And though the silence drags me down,
And sorrow steals my every breath,
I shall surrender to this life,
Only to embrace the loving arms of death.

TIME TRAVELLING MAN

I've been to the future,
And I wasn't surprised,
Or shocked in such a way,
That it opened my eyes,
For as I walked drenched in sorrow,
Along its cold empty streets,
I was reminded of a world,
Trapped in the jaws of defeat.

And what I saw should have shook me,
Right down to the core,
Travelling beyond the anticipation of tomorrow,
Only to be confronted by war,
Where death and destruction,
Were still common place,
Destroying the lives of the hopeful,
With such a merciless grace.

And as I sat,
And I watched,
So my loneliness grew,
Oh how I could have solved all their problems,
With all the things that I knew.
For even though I had travelled from a time before theirs,
Somehow all the wisdom carried forward,
Had become morbidly scarce,
Slowly consumed by the sadness,
By a lifetime of tears,
Placing people's names upon crosses,
Only to add weight to their fears.

For when the silence came,
Before the dawns early rise,
Every mother,
And daughter,
And fatherless child,
Painfully accepted the shadows,
In an attempt to survive,
Embracing the hands of the living,
To mourn the ones who had died.

So I paid my respects,
Whispering a thousand goodbyes,
For although the future looked bleak,
In a while it'd be mine.
But I knew in my heart,
As I returned to my kind,
Using the knowledge I'd gained,
I could educate every mind,
And change what would be,
Before it had even begun,
Because the fights never over,
Until the battle is won,
And peace if it is to prosper,
Can't do it whilst it's holding a gun.

SWIRLING MIST

I came across a Swirling Mist,
Beyond the realms of borrowed time,
It lingered in a cloud like haze,
And consumed the workings of my mind.
For as I stood within its grasp,
A stranger in a foreign place,
Although it bore no eyes as such,
I felt its gaze upon my face.
And as I tried to turn my head,
Its line of sight remained in view,
For everywhere my vision roamed,
So my panic grew and grew.
And though the day was not yet done,
The darkness came and stole its light,
Allowing the painful memories from my past,
The freedom of a second life.
For as I fell down to my knees,
Engulfed in thoughts I used to own,
The familiar face of sorrow smiled,
To remind me of my journey home.

I AWOKE TODAY
IN A WORLD FILLED WITH PAIN

I awoke today in a world filled with pain,
Knowing every teardrop holds no purpose,
Once the sorrow remains,
And as hard as I tried to control every breath,
Still the darkness descended to remind me of death.

For what use are the memories when they cannot be shared?
Lost amongst every lonely tomorrow,
Convinced that nobody cares,
Like the ache in my heart,
Every time I recall,
All the moments I held you,
That will never return.

And the warmth of your smile,
Oh how I'll miss that the most,
Forced to spend a whole lifetime with the living,
Whilst I worship your ghost,
For this shrine that I've made,
The one that carries your name,
Is where I now spend all my time,
Amongst a world filled with pain.

VANCOUVER CITY

It's raining in Vancouver city,
My hearts never happy when you're gone,
You're eyes they sparkle with loving,
Please tell me you'll come on back home.
I've counted the days since you left me,
And even cried at the thought you'd return,
It's so quiet in Vancouver city,
In the place I'll always call home.

FATE

You will come for me,
Of that I am sure,
You will hunt me down,
Until I can hide no more,
I will surrender my body,
Like I've done so before,
But you'll never have my heart,
It's mine,
Not yours!

MY GENERATION

The morning after nothing pill,
The triple latte caffeine thrill,
The cyber sexed cyber kids,
Long term internet relationships.

The daily dose of 'War T.V.',
The director's cut, broadcasting the American dream,
The beauty club has never been so quiet,
Liposuction replaced by the 'Wonder Diet'.

The latest virus is now on-line,
Mutated daily to keep up with the times,
It's ready to download from the web worldwide,
There'll be no problems unlike 'Windows' it will work just fine!

The mobile scene has never been so good,
My newborn child learned to text before she talked,
Her words, bless her are coming on well,
With 500 free each month she keeps in touch with all her friends.

This is my generation,
I know it so well,
Although the world keeps on changing,
You never can tell!

LOVELESS

Emotional pauses linger,
Faint traces reside upon your voice,
A once before beauty,
All battered and crushed.

Physical response surrenders,
Winding down to a timely collapse,
Duplicated feelings,
Muted by passionate lust.

Alternate highways,
Hazard lights blaring in the sun,
Warning signs guide the way,
Up to a point of no return.

NEVER IS MY FOREVER

I'm slowly dying,
Knowing you're my disease,
Praying that your heart will always want me,
In the way that I need.
Filled with guilt and betrayal,
So ashamed of my greed,
Running towards the darkness without caution,
Never wanting to leave.
Just because I'm not crying,
Doesn't mean I can't grieve,
Trading hope for desire,
Till I find my reprieve.
Although your words leave me broken,
I can't deny how I feel,
For without you I am frozen,
And there is no in-between.
Like a constant reminder,
From the second I wake,
He may hold me at night,
But all I see is your face,
Your smile my distraction,
From a life I can't take.

LETTING GO

You've put so much hope in my heart,
That there's no room for confession,
And though I may now worship your path,
It's filled with fear and rejection.

Moving between life and love,
Being pulled in two different directions,
For every breath,
A new step,
Without pause for reflection.

Relying solely on faith,
Never knowing its intentions,
Walking blindly towards the light,
For that one glimpse of affection.

Your fingers interlocked in mine,
Oh how long I've prayed for this distraction!
Accepting desire as my sin,
So as to experience passion.

Eternally denying my angel her wings,
Just for the sake of attraction,
With eyes closed,
I barely breathe,
Waiting for something to happen,
Hiding my smile from this world,
With a vacant expression.

REBORN

Today is the day,
That I learn how to breathe,
Leaving no trace of my sadness,
In this web that I weave.

Tomorrow will come,
Be it all but the same,
Yet the mistakes I have made,
Will no longer remain.

The sun may depart,
Giving way to the rain,
But it won't be my fault,
I won't be to blame.

I shall wear my best smile,
With a pleasant refrain,
And lengthen my stride,
As I walk from this pain,
Knowing there's hope in my heart,
In this world full of change.

And with loves strength to guide me,
I dare not complain,
For upon every new breath,
It whispers your name,
So I carry on believing,
That today is the day.

THE LOOK OF LOVE

The look of love,
Is an overreaction,
Deluding the heart of a stranger,
Into believing the attraction.

How can one simple glance,
Capture the soul deep inside,
Convincing the lonely ever after's,
Whilst they gaze upon its smile.

Forcing even the strongest of minds,
To simply accept as they see,
Without even pausing for reflection,
To acknowledge and breathe.

Never truly understanding,
How everything fits,
Committing completely,
Wholeheartedly,
Within that two second glimpse.

The look of love,
Be it an overreaction,
But how I still find myself looking,
In the hope that it happens,
Sacrificing every inch of my soul,
For just an ounce of its grace,
Knowing I'd cherish it so well,
If it ever looked upon my face.

LITTLE THINGS

The things that don't matter to you,
Would mean the world if they happened to me,
All the hearts you so easily bruise,
Are the ones I still desperately seek.

WISHING STAR

I've placed my love upon a wishing star,
So its light can shine to wherever you are,
Be it day or night,
If you look you'll see,
How I still crave your warmth emotionally.
And no matter the distance,
I know were never far apart,
For there are no boundaries that bind love,
Whilst we hold hope in our hearts.
And this aching inside,
Although it tears at my soul,
Shall become my constant companion,
Until the day you come home.
I will never question its motives,
Or all the scars it creates,
Crying tears beneath the silence,
As my world slowly fades.

Oh my dearest forever!
How I miss what we made,
I find myself lost amongst the lovers,
Hiding this feeling of hate,
Knowing the burden thrust upon me,
Is often sometimes too great.
So please forgive me my darling,
For all my mistakes,
Like forgetting how to breathe,
When I can't touch your face,
Clinging onto every memory with a merciful grace,
Praying the skies shall be your compass,
As you head home with haste,
Upon the hill,
Beyond the sunrise,
Where I eternally await.

I'D LOVE TO

I'd love to awake from the perfect night's dream,
Cradling love in my arms,
Instead of crying these tears,
No longer the victim that the world cannot see,
Making excuses for all the bruises,
Until the pain sets me free.

I'd love to be normal,
And not fear you at all,
Like in bed whilst I sleep,
As your shadow appears at my door,
Always pretending I can't see you,
Like you're not even real,
Another Monster in a story,
Of a book I won't read.

And as hard as I try,
You just can't let me be,
Tasting your breath on my lips,
Wishing I had the courage to scream,
Instead of feeling so helpless,
Whilst you take what you need,
I'm a child for god's sake!
Not a whore from the street!

Will someone please help me for I don't understand?
I keep screaming for him to stop,
But he won't let go of my hands,
Quickly pinning me down with a force I can't fight,
And though my body feels numb,
How he still hurts me inside,
So I lay and I weep,
Until he's finished and gone,
Blood stains mark the sheets,
Where violence sang out its song.

Oh how I hate you blessed Lord,
That you could allow this to happen,
Do I not pray to you enough?
To earn an ounce of compassion,
Never again shall we speak,
Or hold hands in your chapel,
I believed in you once,
But now my faith has been shattered.

I'd love to be someone,
Instead of what I've become,
Playing games with my veins,
Until I find the right one,
Hoping death will take pity,
And quietly swallow me whole,
For life holds no purpose,
Once it's ripped from the soul,
Standing so close to the edge,
I close my eyes,
And I'm gone.

DEUS

Oh tainted world,
You reek of death,
With morbid tongue,
And devils breath,
My heart is stained,
By all your scars,
Like a sacrifice,
I walk a fated path.

Till Kingdom come,
I shall not sleep,
So divine am I,
Even angels weep,
Your sanctuary stands on holy ground,
Its sacred walls,
My eternal shroud.

LOCKDOWN

My heart is at its weakest,
When my life is filled with hope,
That I could wait an eternity for your forgiveness,
If I thought you'd let it show.

Where there's light,
I feel the darkness,
No matter where I hide,
Painting a picture of my sorrow,
With every tear I've ever cried.

If there's an angel here to guide me,
Then my faith has left me blind,
Because I keep searching for salvation,
Just to prove that I'm alive,
Knowing every scar upon my skin,
Reflects the pain I feel inside.

And although the years have brought me memories,
In your arms I'm still a child,
Walking towards the gates of heaven,
Wanting love instead of lies,
Breathing a breath that isn't mine,
In a world I now despise.

TRULY ETERNAL LOVE

Nothing else matters,
When I'm right by your side,
It's like I always know who I am,
Instead of living a life filled with lies.
Happy that heaven finally gave me my angel,
And that it's been you all the while,
A constant reminder of true loves eternal glory,
Every single second you smile.
Always afraid that if I could hold you forever,
There still wouldn't be enough time,
For you are my first,
My last,
You are that mountain I'd climb,
You are my only reason for living,
Oh how I wish that you were mine!
Then I wouldn't feel so empty,
As I lay in bed alone at night,
Because with the thought of you beside me,
Suddenly the whole world would seem alright.
I would close my eyes without worry,
Knowing that when I awake,
There wouldn't be another stolen goodbye,
In a life I cannot take.

ABIDE

It's inside of you,
And it knows your name,
It will play with your heart,
And think it's a game,
Embrace it!
Don't push it away,
For what you'll receive,
Will be worth all the pain.

CLOSE TO YOU

Are you here with me?
Or are you somewhere else?
For when I hold your hand,
You never make a sound.
There's a sadness in your smile,
As if you're crying out for help,
Is your heart still all broken?
As it grieves for someone else,
Or are you scared of finding love?
Is that why you shut me out?

Please share with me your thoughts,
And the feelings that you have,
If you give me a chance,
I promise to always make you proud.
But until that time arrives,
And you realize deep down why,
I will continue to hold you close,
To catch your tear drops when you cry.

ANGEL CHILD

Oh angel child,
As time grows old,
The wings you wore,
Shall haunt my soul,
Upon every stolen summers pass,
I still wear your scars across my heart.
And no one knows,
How hard I've wept,
Beneath sleepless nights of torn regret,
When I close my eyes,
It's your face I see,
A reminder of how we used to be.

For the world has become a mocking bird,
Consuming my every single spoken word,
Like a plague that feeds on mortal flesh,
I dwell deep within its realms of death.
Forever searching for that life we shared,
Holding the hand of a stranger,
Just to show that I cared,
But in my heart my dear angel,
Beyond all the torment and pain,
I'll always cling onto our memories,
Knowing its where you'll remain.
And I shall plead with god,
Until he calls out my name,
Every second,
Of every minute,
Until I can hold you again.

I WATCHED A TREE ONCE

I watched a tree once,
Dancing in the breeze,
It captured my senses,
And brought me to my knees,
It looked so beautiful,
Though it bore no leaves,
It smiled at me with so much love,
That I promised,
Without words,
That I'd never leave.

"I'll never leave..."

PURE

Hold me in your arms,
Close up against the warmth of your heart,
If only once, so I can feel what it would be like,
One second of perfection would last a lifetime,
And whilst in your embrace,
Time will stop,
And we will last forever.

IN MEMORIAM

Here's to the lives of the dearly departed,
Although we may bid you farewell,
Still the memories have lasted,
Knowing that in the place where you sleep,
Shall exist a shrine of our worship,
Awash with colourful flowers,
To remind the whole world you had purpose.

Here's to all the tears,
That we've wept in your name,
Every last drop a constant reminder,
That we'll never get to see you again,
Or touch your face,
And feel the warmth,
In the weight of a smile,
Moving forwards without direction,
As you fall far behind.

Here's to all the moments stolen by fear and regret,
Reaching out towards the hand of your angel,
Till there's nothing else left,
Ready to surrender to god,
Just to lay by your side,
Ignoring every loving solemn warning,
As we break down inside.
Oh how the world loses colour,
Once it's lengthened its stride,
Only allowing us to watch blindly from a distance,
And observe the demise.

Here's to all the brothers,
And their fathers and sons,
And all the mothers,
And their daughters,
And the wives who have suffered.

Here's to all the friends and the long distance lovers,
And all the strangers who have touched the heart of another.

Here's to all the dreamers,
And the souls who had spirit,
May your wings fly you home,
To the heights without limit.

Here's to all the days,
When the sun didn't shine,
Let there be a comfort amongst its shadows,
Until we can find the right time,
Accepting that although we have lost,
It doesn't mean we've forgot,
For 'In Memoriam' we shall honour,
The lives of the fallen,
Singing songs without words,
Eternally calling.

HEART OF GLASS

Placing one hand upon the glass,
Knowing it's for the very last time,
Oh how I always wished you could of wanted me,
Instead of these tears I keep crying.
For my heart was awoken,
From the moment you smiled,
Now it's empty and broken,
And consumed by denial.
And I'm frozen without you,
Barely able to call out your name,
For what kind of love could make me want you,
And then make me hate you the same?
Trapped in a world that hands out hope,
And then cruelly steals it away,
I am no one,
I am nothing,
I'm the remains of the day,
Wanting you to make me feel important,
Instead of pushing me away,
Back to my lonely little room,
Where I'm bound to always stay.

LONELY EVER AFTER

Oh how wonderful it must feel,
To be loved each day anew,
No more lonely ever after's,
Awash with dreams that won't come true.
Watching lovers holding hands,
Wearing smiles upon their face,
Oh how I hate the way they mock me,
And make me feel so out of place.
Forced to hide amongst the shadows,
Wanting something that I crave,
Wishing I could dance beneath the sunshine,
Instead of always living in its shade.
In my lonely little world,
Mourning words I'll never say,
Hoping love will one day find me,
Instead of leading me astray.

BROKEN HEARTED LOVE

I never knew I'd find love,
Until the day I found you,
Or experience the warmth of a morning sunrise,
Beyond a sky of perfect blue.
Captivated by the promise of your smile,
Like it was to be my something brand new,
Oh how I'd always dreamt of becoming yours,
Unaware that you didn't dream of it too.
Why didn't you care about my heart?
Whilst you tore it in two,
Every single tear a stark reminder,
Of all the pain you put me through,
Until I couldn't breathe without thinking,
Did I do something wrong?
Ignoring the ache that dwelled within me,
Screaming the words "you don't belong!"

Blind to the helpfulness of strangers,
Who couldn't bear to hear me crying,
Oh how ashamed I felt that they saw me,
At the moment I was dying,
And then watched with eyes of judgement,
As they passed me on the street,
Never fully understanding how you maimed me,
With your talons of defeat.
I couldn't just dispose of all the memories,
As easily as you,
Swimming against the tide of my own sorrow,
In the search for something new.

Oh why can't I walk amongst the sunshine?
And not this path of no retreat,
Forced to hide amongst the shadows,
Awash with scars upon my feet.
And though you never knew this,
So I guess you'll never know,
Regardless of all the times you tried to hurt me,
I still can't seem to let you go.
And these wounds that try to heal,
The ones you cut in me so deep,
I pick at them in silence,
And quietly watch them as they weep.

TOUCH

Protect your tears,
Keep them safe,
Upon the memories of me,
May they wash your face.
Open your heart,
So that it may breathe,
Show them your colours,
And they will believe.

SACRIFICE

Towards the end of the world,
Amongst the silence of strangers,
I can feel you inside me,
Slowly destroying my angel.

Painted bodies bleed,
Stained by the danger,
Divine is my right,
Stripped down I am nameless.

The weight of you upon me,
Taking what is rightfully mine,
Your pain is my pleasure,
Consuming me one breath at a time.

And if you look close enough,
Every once in a while,
You will see that my tears,
Hide a permanent smile.

EROTIC DESIRES

How I wish you were the one,
Who I could be with tonight,
Tempted by the taste of your skin,
As you lay by my side.
Those dark piercing eyes,
Oh how they tear at my soul!
Until I cannot breathe,
Without knowing,
How far this could go.
Another Second?
Another Minute?
Oh God when will this cease?
I feel your presence,
And without thinking,
I'm ready to surrender complete.
Burned by the fires deep within me,
Awaking every last sin from its sleep,
Wanting you to feed on my cravings,
Until you've devoured every piece.
Attracted to the warmth of your poison,
As though it's flowing through my veins,
Writhing like the dutiful siren,
Torn between passion and pain.
Allowing you the freedom once forbidden,
Behind an illusion of shame,
I'll be your Angel,
I'll be your Devil,
I'll be the whore you can't tame.

Aroused by a feeling deep within me,
I can no longer contain,
And a hunger so ferocious,
That makes me lose self-control,
Closing my eyes,
Soaked in pleasure,
Enslaved by your feverish hold.
Dreaming of erotic desires,
As my shrine slowly weeps,
One hand worshiping deliverance,
Until my lonely heart bleeds,
Allowing me to bathe in its glory,
Whilst I take what I need,
Knowing when I awake from this daydream,
I'll have to hide how I feel,
Secretly thinking of you,
Eternally pretending it's real.

SOMEONE ELSE'S SOMEONE

You shall live in my dreams,
And that's where you will stay,
For I once dreamt that you still loved me,
But someone stole you away.

You may belong to another,
But you'll forever be mine,
Because I can't just let go of all these feelings,
And pretend that I'm fine.

There's not an angel left in heaven,
Who hasn't heard how I've cried,
And for every tear drop I keep bleeding,
It's like another piece of me dies.

I just know if you really knew me,
You would feel the same way,
Then I could wake from this nightmare,
And spare my heart all its pain.

To live a life without loving,
Is like having night without day,
And although I now crave something broken,
It's a lot easier then hearing you say…

"It's over!"

DISTANT LOVE

To my dearest forever,
Wherever you are,
May your love be my compass,
That leads me straight to your heart.
For I lose all direction,
When I'm not by your side,
Lost in a sea of my own sorrow,
Pulled along by the tide.
And the distance that divides us,
Oh how I still travel it alone,
Without sail,
Nor Mast,
To carry me home,
Only the memories we once shared,
That I keep safe inside,
Beneath a sky stained by teardrops,
To mark all the times that I've cried.
And the pain although constant,
Is what keeps me alive,
Refuelling the fire of my desire,
No longer stolen by pride,
So I may return to your shore,
Where the sun always shines,
Wanting to hold you once more,
In the hope you're still mine.

BREAKING TIDES

As I walk along life's endless shore,
Awash with breaking tides of time,
The bitter taste of years gone past,
Consume the workings of my mind.

Beneath foggy haze and swirling mist,
Its golden sands still warm my feet,
But blind am I to jagged stones,
That hide themselves upon its beach.

Their pain albeit short and sharp,
Leave long and everlasting marks,
And yet I tread with caution not,
Undeterred by all the signs to stop.

The shining sun,
My light of hope,
Illuminates the path unknown,
And with every stride I'm closer still,
To where you lay upon the hill.

Your cross of white,
My sacred shrine,
The final piece of you that's mine,
With weary legs and defences down,
I now face my demons homeward bound.

Yet no sword have I that seeks revenge,
Nor words of hate to wield and bend,
But a love to warm my broken heart,
Lending me its courage to continue,
Even though were apart.

For you are the wind against my lonely sails,
You are the colour of the moonlight,
As the skyline turns pale,
You are the words to a song I can never forget,
You are a force beyond all reason consumed by regret.

So forgive me my angel,
If I should arrive to you late,
May heaven close my eyes with its kindness,
Until I can no longer awake.

LITTLE PIECES

And when my time is all but spent,
And heaven marks me with its scent,
I will not cry,
Nor shed a tear,
Or ponder over every stolen year,
For you have shown me life,
And made it complete,
Filled with memories of love,
I will eternally keep.

OH BROKEN HEART

Oh broken heart,
How I pray for thee,
With my arms outstretched,
Down on bended knees,
For these tears I cry,
The ones I dare not own,
Oh how I find a comfort within their sorrow,
Whilst I embrace the unknown.

And though my bearings are lost,
To guide me back home,
I still cling onto the remnants of a love,
That can never be mine,
Knowing as much as I try,
To walk off this pain,
I am grounded by the notion,
That things will never be the same.

TO WHOM IT MAY CONCERN

Oh dearest of affections,
Do not think of me as rude,
For I have listened attentively to your objections,
Whilst harboring this uncontrollable mood.
And as hard as I may try,
To entertain your request,
There still exists an ache within my soul,
I find myself unable to forget.
And though your intentions may be honourable,
The words you speak do not ring true,
For I may not have experienced many lovers,
Albeit but a few,
But when it comes to my heart,
I can honestly say,
That at the mere mention of your name,
It turns the darkest shade of grey.
So forgive me if you can,
Although you do not see it yet,
There'll come a day you thank me so,
For I'll have saved you from regret,
Because the love I gave you last,
The one you swore you'd always keep,
Is but a stranger in your presence,
Just like the way I'll always be.

LOVES ETERNAL STRUGGLE

Oh my wanting ray of silent hope,
How my heart does break before your dawn,
For a simple man was I born once,
Unblemished by the scars that scorn.
And yet this soul I carry forth,
A reminder of my childhood gone,
How it speaks in words I cannot see,
Like that of sorrows silent tongue.
And as I bow my lowly head,
Consumed by faiths eternal cross,
Before me stands a flower still,
Adorned with loves forgiving gloss.
Its silken leaves beyond my reach,
Oh how I've longed to touch them so,
Their golden warmth upon my cheek,
Enslaves me with a loving glow.
And as I fall down to my knees,
Awash with tears that never come,
I close my eyes to broken thoughts,
That fade beneath the setting sun.
For every time I think of you,
Be it twilights dusk or mornings hue,
I die bereft of wantant things,
Like an angel of mercy,
Falling for the promise of love without the safety of wings,

'I struggle'.

ETERNALLY IN LOVE

You give me hope,
When life offers me none,
Holding my hand through all the bad times,
Until the good ones return,
So please forgive me my angel,
For I haven't forgot,
I will always love you without question,
And pray to god,
That my heart never stops.

LOVE HURTS

I'm like a stranger in a familiar place,
So annoyed with myself,
That I can't bear to look at your face,
Or acknowledge your tears,
The ones that I've made,
Knowing I'm no longer a man,
Well, at least not today.

I can now only pray for tomorrow to come,
With a hope that you'll wake,
And forgive what I've done,
And smile like you used to,
Before all the pain made you numb.

But when you promised to love me,
You just can't take that away,
I won't let you leave,
So you'll just have to stay.
And if anyone should ask,
Why you're always afraid,
Or how for each bruise you now hide,
Your life gets delayed,
Please don't tell them the truth,
Because I know things have changed,
And for every scar upon your skin,
I'm eternally ashamed.

GOOD ADVICE

Listen to me child,
For my words are universal,
You can't just bury your head in the sand,
Pretending life's the rehearsal.

Remove all the weeds from your path,
Before their roots become dirty,
And fill it with colourful plants,
So that the sunshine has purpose.

Gather the rain from the clouds,
So you shall never grow thirsty,
Savouring the taste in your mouth,
Taking strength from its waters.

As you take from this world,
Always share half with the needy,
Knowing with what you'll receive in return,
You shall never grow greedy.

Remember to be kind to your friends,
As it will earn their respect,
For today is not the day,
To dwell on regret,
So replace the sorrow for tomorrow,
And forgive or forget,
Holding hands with your loved ones,
Because without them what's left?

So take my advice,
And give it some thought,
I shall be watching you from heaven,
Ready to lend my support,
Giving back hope to the hopeless,
Teaching those who aren't taught,
Forever the Angel,
I'll be eternally yours.

LITTLE GIRL BY THE SIDE OF THE ROAD

Oh little girl how you sit by the side of the road,
Convinced that life has forgot you,
And that you're all on your own,
For as the cars pass you by I feel your hope slowly fade,
And your eyes although open hold a permanent gaze.
Tell me where do you come from and what is your name?
I hear you crying and it kills me to learn of your pain.
Did your mummy not want you?
Or your daddy the same?
What of your brothers and sisters?
Oh it's all such a shame!

And I wish you could see me as I sit by your side,
Wanting to wrap my love around your heart,
Until you remember how to smile.
And your tears though they haunt you,
May they no longer be,
For you're just a child seeking refuge,
Harbouring the premise of a dream,
Wanting someone to want you,
And gently reach out their hand.
But until that time arrives however long it may be,
I'll always stand where you stand,
And breathe whilst you breathe,
Because you'll never feel at home,
When you belong to the streets,
Unnoticed,
Undernourished,
Existing down at the depths of peoples feet.

I bet you wish things could be different,
Every time you close your eyes and sleep,
My Angel…
I love you…
And that's a promise I'll always keep.

AFRAID TO FALL

Upon a Look,
A gaze,
You consume me whole,
That I could give my heart to something,
That I dare not own.
You test my faith,
Like its nothing at all,
Please help me,
Hold my hand,
For without you by my side,
I'm too afraid to fall.

FOREVER FRIENDS

There's not a single word left to say,
That hasn't already been said,
You've been a part of my life,
Since the day we first met.

With our paths intertwined,
By a bond that stays strong,
I have no doubt in my heart,
As to where I belong.

And when times have been tough,
You're always right by my side,
Giving me strength,
Making me smile.

When I prayed for an angel,
I know heaven heard my request,
Because to have you as a friend,
Reminds me how much I've been blessed.

Although the futures unwritten,
May it be filled with your dreams,
So that each new memory you share,
Can show the whole world how you feel.

As the 'father of the bride'
On this very special day,
I shall give to you a gift,
That can never be replaced.

'LOVE'

LIFE WITHOUT YOUR LOVE

To my dearest forever after,
Wherever you may be,
As I walk this path without you,
Oh how I lose the will to breathe.
Lost in burning fields of sorrow,
Beyond the vastness of the sea,
I'd sell my soul to god tomorrow,
If it brought you back to me.
Begging angels for their forgiveness,
In the hope they'd understand,
Wanting love to become my saviour,
As it guides me with its hand.
And then I wouldn't feel so helpless,
Whilst I cry myself to sleep,
Watching dreams that held such promise,
Slipping just beyond my reach.
For today shall be the day,
Once the sun sets in the skies,
That will haunt me come the morning,
Without you laying by my side.
Whispering goodnight to the long departed,
Still too afraid to say goodbye,
Just another lonely hearted traveller,
Who once held love,
And watched it die.

I WONDER

I often wonder whilst I walk along life's empty roads,
Beyond its busy city limits,
Towards the houses in their rows,
For when I see a broken man,
Tears clearly streaming down his face,
I wonder,
How does he recall loves smile?
Without the warmth of its embrace.
And then I find myself believing,
That whomever he now grieves,
Shall always haunt him with each waking breath,
Like a pain that never leaves.
And all the memories they once shared,
Tell me, where do they go?
Does he awake upon an average day,
Forgetting all the things he used to know,
Until he's nothing but a shadow of the man he used to be,
Following a line without direction,
Blind to things he'll never see.
And then I wonder if I stopped,
Instead of walking right on past,
And took the time to tell him sorry,
For all the things that never last,
I wonder,
Would it really matter?
That I acknowledged how he felt,
Or would his scars be so ingrained within,
That he'd barely know himself,
Unaware that right before him,
Exists an angels hand of help,
Eternally awaiting until the moment,
He finds the strength to reach on out,
I wonder.

LOVE SONG

I wrote you a love song,
But I've forgotten all the words,
I worked on it for ages,
Yet I can't recall a verse.

I didn't write it down,
Just in case you saw it first,
You probably think I'm foolish,
And that just makes it even worse.

I hope you can forgive me,
And look beyond my big mistake,
I only wanted to tell you that I love you,
But all my words have been misplaced.

UNRENDERED AFFECTION

If I should die before we meet,
Who'll tell your heart that I have gone?
For all the words we never spoke,
Are lost to where they once belonged.
And though our paths may never cross,
I start each day with hope renewed,
Knowing every stranger that I pass,
I'm one step close to finding you.
And though my eyes no longer see,
Oh how my voice still calls your name,
Forced to walk till kingdom come,
Enslaved by loves eternal pain.
For what am I without your grace?
When faith has gone and nothings left,
Pleading with a god who gave me life,
To remove this ache inside my chest.
Oh tell me angel where you roam?
For I have searched the whole world through,
Sharing all my nights with restless thoughts,
Instead of spending time with you.
And the thing that hurts the most,
That I have carried all along,
Is if I should die before we meet,
Who'll tell your heart that I have gone?

SLOW ROAD TO RUIN

It's a slow road to ruin,
So can you cut me some slack!
I'll get to where I'm supposed to be going,
And there'll be no more looking back.
You may well call me a quitter,
But I can promise you this,
I'll keep walking towards the firestorm,
Until I reach its Abyss.
Carrying this burden upon my shoulders,
Like a beacon of light,
Ready to shine it amongst the doubters,
Who came along to watch the fight.

So come on all you sinners!
With all your words of hate and spite,
Go on and hurt me with your betrayal,
So you can sleep with ease at night.
Scar my skin with your indifference,
Pull me down to where you preach,
Cover all the ears of those who listen,
Remove the freedom from their speech.

For I am an army without knowing,
I am the words you'll never speak,
I may be on this road to reap my ruin,
But it leaves no marks upon my feet.
And tomorrow there'll be sunshine,
Regardless of today,
Because with Hope and Faith inside me,
I shall never lose my way.

INNOCENT HEART

Betrothed to another,
I'm denied of your touch,
Yet I still find myself wanting,
Like an emotional crutch.
Whenever you're around me,
I don't know where to look,
All these feelings I hold sacred,
Can never be took.
Devoured by silence,
I submit to its fate,
With my innocence lost,
Only my heart may you break.

HOPE

Whenever I feel myself falling,
The ground rushing towards me fast,
It's always you that I think of,
My eyes closed to the dark,
For you give me my wings,
Even though were far apart,
And in an instant I'm flying,
Wearing hope upon my heart.

IMMOBILE

You're not where I left you,
Like you were in the past,
That familiar feeling,
Knowing I belonged in your arms.

Tell me where did you go?
Do you dwell in the dark?
Because my heart needs its keeper,
Not a life filled with scars.

Bound eternal to a place,
That the light cannot reach,
My solace remains stolen,
By a strangers reprieve,
And endurance knows its boundaries,
Once I'm brought to my knees.

I keep looking in the mirror,
Wanting the reflection to change,
But with all this blood on my hands,
It's too late to be saved.

So forgive me my sins,
And the fact that I'm weak,
For my body now lays broken,
Holding hands with deceit,
Robbed by a world,
Where true love is the thief!

SCARS FOR AN ANGEL

In my fragile state,
There's always a potential for harm,
Because the smile I show the world,
Hides all the cuts upon my arms.

The wounds will always heal,
But they leave behind their scars,
And I'm reminded as I cry,
Of all the pain left in my heart.

If there's a beauty deep within me,
Tell me where does it sleep?
For I'm so tired of being something ugly,
That no one ever needs.

I keep praying that an angel,
Will wake me from this dream,
But it's hard to believe in heaven,
When I have no self-esteem.

If I told you all my reasons,
I know you'd never understand,
I'm not asking for forgiveness,
Just a friend to hold my hand.

BROKEN HEARTED

Is there a reason you didn't want me?
Or should I have guessed that for myself?
Because every time you chose to ignore me,
All you left me with was doubt.

Couldn't you hear the sound as my heart broke?
Or see the tears that you put in my eyes?
I bet you didn't care how much you could hurt me,
As you filled me with your lies.

I kept on waiting every day for your phone call,
But of course it would never come,
All my friends kept trying to warn me,
But I always told them that they were wrong.

I only wanted somebody to love me,
And I prayed that you were the one,
But I guess because of my desperation,
You thought you'd have some fun.

All my family and friends have disowned me,
Because of all the hurtful things that I've said,
But I wonder how much they will want me,
When they learn that I am dead!

I WALK ALONE

In silent steps,
I walk alone,
My arms outstretched,
Towards the sky,
The warming sun,
A distant friend,
Reminds me of the hope love brings.
For when I smile,
It never rains,
And the clouds return,
From where they came,
So that every time I think of you,
This familiar path,
Becomes my something new.
And the trees that stretch beyond my reach,
Every silver ash and golden birch,
Oh how I marvel at their dainty leaves,
Awash with dreams of every passing bird.
For no beauty in the world compares,
To the freedom found within the open air,
Soaring high above the clouds at speed,
Feeling the wind upon your feathers,
Whilst you dance amongst the breeze.
And one day I know that's where I'll be,
For these wings I hide shall set me free,
And though I walk alone with scars upon my feet,
I shall always think of you as mine,
Until the day we finally meet.

STRANGER

Say anything to me,
Just don't say goodbye,
Because I can't feel you like I used to,
Deep down inside.
I've a fragile heart,
The kind that's easily bruised,
And I keep praying that someone will save me,
I hope that someone is you.

MY WINDOW

My world doesn't end at your window,
It ends when I whisper "Good night",
The tears that I cry won't truly show,
The feelings I hold deep down inside.

My world doesn't end at your window,
It ended as the rain fell last night,
Your last breath as I held you,
Through my tears as I kissed you,
"I love you" my angel,
"Good night".

I DANCED A MERRY DANCE TODAY

I danced a merry dance today,
As the sun came out and shone my way,
All the clouds above so dark and grey,
Floated beyond the horizon without delay.
And the blowing winds,
Once a raging storm,
Became but a whisper of silence,
Amongst the breaking dawn,
For today I learned what I've always known,
That even when there's no one around,
I'm never completely alone.
And as I closed my eyes,
I slowly moved unheard,
Every single step,
Like a spoken word,
For the world can seem such a peaceful place,
When fear is consumed by its loving grace,
Turning all my lonely thoughts into a gentle sway,
Oh how I danced a merry dance today.

EVERMORE

I shall remain where you once left me,
With all this hope held in my heart,
And pray the memories that I now cling to,
Will be enough whilst were apart.
There's not a soul who will believe me,
Whenever I say that you'll return,
It's like the faith they once belonged to,
Has been taken from this world.

I can still feel your love within me,
Though I'd never let it show,
Because it reminds me that I'm lonely,
And how it hurt to let you go.
The distance that divides us,
Still devours all my strength,
There's a girl inside this woman,
Crying tears since the day that you went.

So if you're thinking of me,
Wherever you may be,
Just close your eyes and dream of heaven,
And an angel you will see.

FRIENDS

What is it in our mind,
That leads us to believe,
That people can love us,
As they use us and leave.

And what's in our hearts,
That needs it so bad,
When we find something new,
We always seem to crave what we had.

And what of our bodies,
The physical touch,
When one night of passion,
Is often too much.

But who is it that helps,
When the relationship ends,
More important than love,
These people are our friends.

WORDS

I never go looking,
They always find me,
As I write them down,
It becomes harder to breathe.
Overwhelmed by their sadness,
I'm tortured by grief,
That I could surrender my soul,
For an ounce of reprieve.
So divine is my devil,
That I'm required to submit,
My obligation surpasses,
All this pain and regret.
Consumed in a sentence,
Devoured by a word,
I'm resigned to my fate,
Unnoticed,
Unheard.

I SAW HER

I saw her,
I saw the poor girl lying on the floor,
All broken and bruised,
Her hands reaching,
Grabbing the air,
Looking for hope,
Screaming out so loud.
I could hear her heart breaking in her voice,
Crying out for the love of her 'mummy',
I wanted to tell her to think only of angels,
In the hope that they would take her away from this dark place,
So her spirit could be protected by her innocence.

"Stop…please stop…I beg of you…"

I wanted to hold her,
Till she could cry no more,
To apologise for you,
But I couldn't,
I felt hopeless,
I froze,
Falling powerless to my knees,
Overcome by tears.

I remember the darkness and how it taunted me so,
I remember it every time I close my eyes,
Every time I see her pretend to smile.

"Forgive me"

OH WHAT A WONDROUS THOUGHT LOVE CAN BE

Oh what a wondrous thought love can be,
As it pulls you in,
Until you can barely breathe,
With every second spent in its warm embrace,
Oh how the world can seem like a perfect place.
And regardless of the time of day,
Oh how its presence never leaves me,
Or fades away,
For I know each time it calls my name,
There lives a longing within my soul,
I can't easily explain.
So I await every day,
Whilst I bathe in its breeze,
Overpowered by desire,
I'm often brought to my knees,
And the tears that I cry,
Are not of sorrow or pain,
But of hope,
And Joy,
Knowing love will greet me again.

FROM ACROSS THE ROOM

From across the room,
I always feel so small,
My body like a starless night,
Before the early mornings call.
This sea of strangers,
Oh how they hide me away,
My words devoured upon every breath,
Until there's nothing left to say.
And I envy what they see,
In their neatly fashioned rows,
Feeling the fires within me burn,
Whilst my hunger for you grows.
And yet I'm forced to look away,
My vision bereft of any view,
Never wanting another empty tomorrow,
When each day begins a new,
Quietly watching you forever,
From across the room,
Knowing I'll always feel invisible and broken,
Every time I look at you.

DROWNED

I'm surrounded by chaos,
Everywhere that I turn,
It's like I can't breathe for a second,
Without someone draining my Worth.

Every time we now speak,
I'm sucked into your world,
Where all the silence is broken,
And the pains even worse.

Why do you despise me so much?
As you feed at my wounds,
How can all the love I once cherished,
Become so easily bruised.

You have made me a stranger,
In a place I once knew,
With my sacred heart stolen,
All my strength is consumed,
And I can't fight it any longer,
When my sanctuary's ruined.

I PROMISE

I promise to remember you every day,
Even after all the well-wishers have departed,
And gone their separate way.

I promise to recall every moment we shared,
Placing a constant rose upon your grave,
To show the whole world how I cared.

I promise to remind everyone that you lived,
And that your life is just as important,
Although you now no longer exist.

I promise to be honest,
When people ask how I feel,
Instead of pretending that I'm fine,
And that the pain isn't real.
For these tears that I wear,
I won't hide them away,
May they forever stain my soul,
As I live and breathe each day.

I promise to endure a lifetime alone,
Knowing the second god calls my name,
I'll finally be on my way home.

I promise all these things,
Because I know in my heart,
The next time I see you again,
It will be as though we were never torn apart.

ANGELUS

I am nothing more nor am I nothing less,
I am every single spoken word you've ever left unsaid,
I am clarity just beyond the light,
I am emerald green and opal white.

I am your last call of the day,
I am your early morning rise,
I am that feeling you get when you smile,
Deep down inside.

I am 'Eros' and 'Aphrodite',
I am known by many names,
But most of all I'm here,
And by your side I shall remain.

Your lips no longer may I kiss,
And though your touch has gone away,
Upon your memories and your dreams,
I still love you every day.

MORNING GLORY

Oh morning glory,
How you always greet me so,
And though I would normally surrender to your splendour,
Today my whole world just seems so cold.
For the shadows that consume me,
Oh how they love to watch me bleed,
Until I find myself lost within each moment,
Like a hostage on my knees.
And though I always search for your sunshine,
Between the clouds up in the sky,
Even the promise of a perfectly formed rainbow,
Cannot erase these teardrops from my eyes.
For however loud I scream,
All my words are never heard,
Beginning each day albeit new,
Like I'm moving in reverse,
Carrying this ache within my chest,
Every single step I take,
Knowing when I close my eyes at night,
My dreams will haunt me till I wake.
For the glory of the morning as it arrives in all its grace,
Makes the fear within me grow,
Until my body starts to shake,
One finger wrapped around the trigger,
Like a reminder of my fate,
But as the empty barrel clicks,
And sorrow fills me with its hate,
I breathe another silent breath,
In a life I cannot take.

IN BETWEEN THE LINES

In between the lines,
I slowly drift,
Lost amongst my thoughts without knowing,
Even before they exist.
And although you cannot see me,
In the way that I'd like,
I still wait beyond the shadows,
Awash with tears I cannot cry.
And the silence consumes me,
Without pause for regret,
Caught in the tide of my own sorrow,
Unallowed to forget,
For the pain never stops,
From the moment I awake,
And these scars slowly worsen,
Every time my heart breaks.
For what am I without purpose?
When it's all that I crave,
Holding this sword within my hands,
Like I'm supposed to be brave.
And my army of supporters,
Tell me where do they hide?
For I now stand on my own,
As I slowly drift,
In between the lines.